THE LOST™ CHRONICLES Part 2

Based on the *Lost* Series One companion book by Mark Cotta Vaz

Based on the following Episodes:
111 (Written by Carlton Cuse and Javier Grillo-Marxuach)
112 (Written by David Fury)
113 (Written by Damon Lindelof)
114 (Written by Drew Goddard)
115 (Written by Javier Grillo-Marxuach and Leonard Dick)
116 (Written by David Fury and Brent Fletcher)
117 (Written by Carlton Cuse and Damon Lindelof)
118 (Written by Janet Tamaro)
119 (Written by Leonard Dick)
120 (Story by Javier Grillo-Marxuach; Teleplay by Edward Kitsis and Adam Horowitz)
121 (Written by Damon Lindelof and Carlton Cuse)
122 (Written by Damon Lindelof and Carlton Cuse)

LEVEL 3

SCHOLASTIC

Adapted by: Rod Smith

Publisher: Jacquie Bloese

Commissioning Editor: Helen Parker

Editor: Matthew Hancock

Designer: Susen Vural

Cover layout: Emily Spencer

Picture research: Emma Bree

Photo credits: Cover and interior photos courtesy of ABC Studios and © American Broadcasting Companies, Inc.
Pages 72 & 73: AM Corporation/Alamy; M. Borchi/Atlantide Phototravel/Corbis.
Pages 76 & 77: Mary Evans Picture Library, D. Noble/ Alamy; D. Sternoczky/SUFOI/Fortean/Topfoto; AP Photo.

Originally published in the United States of America and Canada by Hyperion as THE LOST CHRONICLES. This abridged edition published by arrangement with Hyperion.

Published by Scholastic Ltd 2008

Mary Glasgow Magazines / Scholastic Ltd
Euston House
24 Eversholt Street
London
NW1 1DB

Printed in Singapore.

CONTENTS PAGE

Several weeks ago *Oceanic Flight 815* from Sydney to Los Angeles crashed on an island. These are the main survivors:

Jack is a handsome young doctor. He had gone to Australia to find his father. He was too late. His father had died. Jack was taking his body home to Los Angeles. Jack is a natural leader. He is sensible, brave and intelligent.

Kate is a beautiful young woman – and a criminal who escaped to Australia from the USA. When the plane crashed, she was returning to Los Angeles with a police guard. Kate is clever, popular and brave.

Locke is a quiet, older man. He had gone to Australia to join an adventure group. The group leader wouldn't take him because he was in a wheelchair, so he was returning home. After the crash, he was able to walk again and became very good at hunting. He seems to understand the island and the other survivors.

Sayid had been an Iraqi soldier. In Iraq he had helped a close friend, Nadia, escape from prison. He escaped to Australia then took the flight to Los Angeles to find Nadia. He is strong, intelligent, brave and very good with technology.

Sawyer is often rude, selfish and angry. Sawyer had gone to Australia to kill a criminal who destroyed his family. He collects useful things from the plane. If one of the survivors needs something, Sawyer often has it.

Claire is single and expecting a baby. She was flying to Los Angeles to give her baby to another couple. A few days ago Claire disappeared – a strange man called Ethan Rom attacked her and took her away.

Charlie had gone to Australia to visit his brother, Liam. He wanted Liam to rejoin their band. He refused so Charlie was returning home. Soon after the crash Locke helped him to stop taking drugs. He finds life difficult without drugs. It is even more difficult without Claire as they were becoming very close.

Hurley had gone to Australia to discover the meaning behind some special numbers. No one knows much about Hurley's past. On the island he's just a big, friendly guy who likes people to have a good time.

Jin was flying to Los Angeles on a business trip with his wife, Sun. They are both from Korea. Sun's father only agreed to their marriage if Jin worked for him. In his job, Jin had to do things he thought were wrong. He kept these things secret from Sun. This made their life together very difficult.

Sun was on the plane with her husband, Jin. Sun believed that Jin had done some terrible things while working for her father. She had planned to leave Jin at the airport. But when Jin showed her a flower as a sign of his love, she couldn't do it. On the island Sun has made a garden with plants for food and medicine.

Michael was bringing his son, Walt, back home to the USA. He wants to be close to his son, but he doesn't know how. He doesn't like Walt spending time with Locke.

Walt is ten years old. He was living in Australia with his mother when she died. His parents didn't live together. His father, Michael, was taking him back home to the USA when the plane crashed. Walt doesn't really know his father. He prefers his dog, Vincent, and Locke, who teaches him about the island.

Boone was flying back to Los Angeles with his sister, Shannon. Shannon and Boone are always disagreeing. He is a kind young man who cares about other people. He wants to do something useful on the island.

Shannon was returning home with Boone after leaving her Australian boyfriend. When she's not being rude to Boone, she spends her time sunbathing. She just wants to be rescued from the island as quickly as possible.

PLACES

It is a beautiful island somewhere in the south Pacific Ocean. No one knows exactly where it is. But everyone agrees it is a dangerous and mysterious place. There are wild boar and polar bears in the forest, and a strange 'thing' that can kill. The island touches everyone's deepest fears and secrets. It opens the past and changes the present. And who are 'The Others' that also live on the island? Can the survivors escape?

THE LOST™ CHRONICLES Part 2

PROLOGUE

Almost a month ago our flight from Sydney to Los Angeles crashed on an island in the south Pacific. Many people died, but I survived along with forty-eight other people. During our time here, strange things have happened to me. I see and hear everything, even people's thoughts. Every day I write a chronicle about what the people do, what they think and how they survive.

The island is very beautiful and we know we are lucky to be alive. But it's no ordinary island - and most of the survivors have not had ordinary lives.

Our leader, Jack, is the only doctor on the island. He's a very sensible guy but even he has started to see things here. Sometimes he sees his father's ghost in the forest. He thinks that the death of his father was his fault.

Kate is a very beautiful woman and Jack likes her a lot. A rough guy called Sawyer finds her attractive, too. Only Jack, Hurley and Sawyer know that Kate was a criminal. She was with a police guard on the plane. The guard had a metal suitcase with him. It was full of guns. It also had a toy plane inside it. After the crash Kate found the suitcase and Jack helped her to open it. She didn't care about the guns; all she wanted was the toy plane. At first she told Jack that it belonged to the man she loved. Then she told him it belonged to the man she killed.

Locke is one of the strangest people on the island. The other survivors don't know that he was in a wheelchair before the crash. After the crash, he was able to walk again. Locke believes that the island gave him this gift. He seems to understand the island and the other survivors better than anyone. He isn't afraid of the huge thing that attacks people in the forest or the strange polar bears.

A young guy called Boone is spending a lot of time with Locke. They go out hunting boar together, but I know that they aren't really hunting. They've found something very unusual in the forest - a mysterious hatch. Locke doesn't want to tell anyone about it - not yet.

Locke has been very good to Charlie. Charlie was in a band and used to take drugs. With Locke's help Charlie has given them up. Life without drugs isn't easy for him and it's even worse since Claire disappeared. Charlie was getting very close to her and misses her very much.

We are all really worried about Claire. She is expecting a baby and is in great danger. A man called Ethan Rom took her. We discovered that Ethan wasn't on our plane when it crashed. No one knows who he is or why he's taken Claire. All we know is that we want her back.

We are very lucky to have Sayid in our group. He was a soldier in Iraq and is brilliant with technology. Soon after we crashed on the island he tried to send a message using the radio from the plane. Unfortunately he couldn't because another message was stopping it. It said in French, 'Please help me. I'm alone on the island. The others are dead. It killed them all.' This message is sixteen years old and it just plays over and over again.

Another time Sayid was in the forest when he fell into a trap. He woke up in a strange camp. Suddenly, he heard the voice of a Frenchwoman. She told him that her name was Danielle. She had been on the island for sixteen years. The rest of her group had died of a terrible illness. She talked about 'The Black Rock', 'The Others' and her baby son, Alex. Sayid thought she was crazy and he managed to escape from her. But as he walked back through the forest he heard whispers in the dark ...

Maybe there really are 'Others' on the island. What is 'The Black Rock'? What happened to Danielle's son, Alex?

These are just some of the island's many mysteries. I will try to record them all.

CHAPTER 1 SHANNON'S STORY

We've been on the island for a few weeks now. We have a camp on the beach and another at the caves. All the survivors are starting to get to know each other. It's interesting to watch as some people make friends and others become enemies.

Right now I'm watching Shannon and Sayid at the beach camp. They are becoming very friendly. But Shannon's brother, Boone, doesn't like it at all. Maybe because Sayid was an Iraqi soldier?

This morning, Boone walked up to Sayid and shouted, 'Stay away from my sister!' I don't really understand why Boone cares so much. He doesn't seem to like his sister. They disagree all the time.

A little later, the older man, Locke, told Boone not to make an enemy of Sayid. 'We need Sayid on our side,' he said.

Locke understands people better than anyone. He knows that Sayid is strong and brave. He will be useful for our survival.

Boone is spending a lot of time with Locke at the moment. Every day they go into the forest to hunt boar. But each evening they return to camp with no boar. The others are starting to ask questions. Are they really hunting out there?

Locke and Boone have a secret. They have found a strange hatch in the forest. They want to know what is inside this hatch. But they can't open it. Every day, they go back into the forest to work out how to get inside. They haven't told anyone about this. Locke thinks the other survivors won't understand and might upset his plans.

✈

Shannon is the most interested in Locke and Boone's journeys into the forest.

'She doesn't believe we're hunting,' Boone told Locke as they sat by the hatch.

Locke was mixing something up in a bowl. It looked like thick cream. He told Boone that getting inside the hatch was more important than what Shannon or anyone else believed. 'Anyway, why do you care about Shannon so much?' he asked.

'She's my sister. She's … special,' Boone replied.

Boone's thoughts returned to the day he arrived in Sydney from Los Angeles. Shannon had phoned and asked him to rescue her.

She had left to go and live with a man called Brian in Sydney, Australia. Now she had finished with him and she needed money to make him go away. It wasn't the first time she had phoned Boone like this. She was always disappearing with new boyfriends, then asking Boone to come and get her when things went wrong.

But this time Shannon and Brian tricked Boone. Boone met Brian and gave him a cheque for $50,000. Later, he went to get Shannon from Brian's house. Brian told him that Shannon was staying with him – and they were keeping the money. Brian knew that Shannon wasn't Boone's real sister. She was his stepsister. When Shannon's father died, Boone's mother didn't want to know her. His mother was very rich and she only gave money to Boone. Now it was time for Shannon to have some of that money.

Boone was very angry and he fought with Brian. Brian was a lot stronger and won easily. Shannon was upset about the fight. But it didn't change anything. There was nothing Boone could do. In the end, he left and went back to his hotel.

That evening, there was a knock on the door of his room. It was Shannon. She was very upset. Brian had left her and taken the money. She said she was sorry, but she knew Boone would help her because he was in love with her. Boone tried to say this wasn't true, but Shannon moved closer. They started to kiss …

Locke told Boone he could tell Shannon about the hatch if he wanted. They stood up and Boone turned to go back to camp. Suddenly, Locke hit Boone hard on the back of the head. Boone fell to the ground unconscious.

✈

Boone woke up tied to a tree. Locke was sitting with the strange cream in the bowl. He put some of the cream on Boone's injury. 'This will stop it turning bad,' he said.

Boone felt sleepy. 'Why are you doing this to me?' he asked. Locke told him that it was time to let go.

'Let go of what?' Boone wondered. He jumped as Locke's knife flew past him. It stuck into the ground about a metre from his feet. Locke turned to go.

'You can't leave me here!' Boone cried.

'When you want to escape badly enough, you will,' said Locke. Then he left.

Boone tried hard to reach the knife but the ropes cut into his body. The pain was too much.

Suddenly, he heard a scream for help. It was Shannon. Seconds later, he heard something that sounded like a dangerous creature. It was the huge thing that lived in the forest. It had killed before and Shannon was in terrible danger.

In great pain, Boone finally managed to reach the knife. He cut through the ropes and ran to Shannon. She was tied to a tree. There was no time for questions. The thing was coming. He cut Shannon free and they ran off through the forest.

It was getting closer. They hid quickly in the middle of a circle of trees. They were really frightened and held onto each other tightly. They couldn't see the thing, but they knew it wasn't far away.

When they felt sure that it had gone, they left their hiding place. As they hurried through the forest, Shannon shouted angrily at Boone, 'What did you do to Locke? What made him do this?'

Boone told Shannon about the hatch in the ground. But she had no time to be surprised. The thing suddenly appeared from nowhere, picked Shannon up and disappeared through the trees. 'Shannon!' Boone screamed and tried to follow them.

A few minutes later, he found her. She was lying covered in blood by the side of a small river. Boone ran over to her. He was too late. She was dead. He held Shannon in his arms and cried.

Meanwhile, Kate and the Korean woman, Sun, were having a much more peaceful time. They were working together in the garden Sun had made. Kate liked working there. It was quiet and no one could ask her about her past. While they were digging Kate often talked to herself, thinking that Sun didn't understand English.

Sun's eyes were on the ground when Kate said something. Suddenly, Sun looked up and laughed.

Kate looked at Sun in surprise. 'You understood me!' she said. 'You speak English!'

Sun told her it was true. The only other person on the island that knew she understood English was Michael. Her husband, Jin, didn't know. She didn't want Jin to find out.

'Please don't tell him,' she said.

'Don't worry,' Kate replied. 'I can keep a secret.'

✈

It's the end of the day and we're sitting around the camp fire. Suddenly, Boone races into the camp and tries to attack Locke. 'You killed Shannon!' he screams.

Locke protects himself easily from Boone. 'So where's the blood?' he asks calmly.

Boone looks down at his arms where they held Shannon. He was sure that there was blood on them before. But they are completely clean. Locke then tells him to look over at the camp fire. When he looks, he sees Shannon talking to Sayid. Her death wasn't real! He can't believe it.

Locke explains, 'That cream I put on your head. It was a kind of drug. It makes you see things. How did you feel when you found Shannon dead?'

'I felt like a great weight had been taken from me.'

'Yes!' says Locke with a smile. 'It's time to let go, Boone. Follow me ...'

The two men get up and disappear into the forest.

CHAPTER 2 LOOKING FOR WALT

This morning Michael was up early looking for Walt, his ten-year-old son. He asked Charlie if he had seen him.

'No, sorry,' Charlie replied. He was also looking for something – Claire's things. He really missed Claire. He wanted to find her diary. He knew it was important to her.

When Jack arrived at the beach, Michael asked him about Walt.

'I saw him back at the caves,' said Jack. 'I think he was taking Vincent for a walk.'

✈

But Walt wasn't walking his dog. He was with Locke and Boone. Locke was teaching him how to throw a knife. At first, Walt couldn't do it very well.

'Think very hard about what you want to hit,' Locke told him.

Walt followed the advice. He threw the knife and it stuck in a tree.

'Yes, I did it!' shouted Walt. He and Locke were happy.

But their smiles soon disappeared when Michael arrived. He saw the knife and was very angry. 'Are you crazy?' he shouted at Locke. 'Knives are dangerous. Don't teach my boy how to use them!' Then he ordered Walt to take Vincent back to the beach camp.

Locke asked Michael if he really knew Walt. If he did, he would know that Walt was different. He could be treated more like a man, not a boy.

This made Michael even angrier. 'Stay away from my son,' he said. 'And me!'

As Michael walked away he thought about Locke's

words. One thing was true. He didn't know his son very well. But it wasn't his fault. He had never had the chance.

Michael remembered a time in New York just before Walt was born. He was buying Walt's first bed with Susan, Walt's mother. Those were good times. But they didn't last. Michael wanted to be an artist but often he worked as a builder just to earn money. When Walt was about one year old the building work stopped. Soon after this, Susan was offered a good job in Amsterdam. They weren't married and Michael couldn't stop her leaving with Walt.

A few months after Susan left, Michael called her from a phone box. She told him she was in love with her new boss, Brian Porter. Michael told her that they couldn't keep Walt. He was coming to Amsterdam to get him. He threw the phone

down angrily and stepped into the road. He didn't check the traffic and was hit by a car. He was lucky to be alive, but had to spend the next year in hospital.

He was very surprised when Susan came to the hospital one day to see him. But surprise soon turned to anger. Susan told him that she was marrying Brian and that Brian wanted to be Walt's father.

Not long after this visit, Susan moved with Brian and Walt to Sydney. Michael spent the next nine years away from his son. He wrote many letters to Walt, but his son never replied.

Then one day Brian arrived at Michael's home. Susan had died suddenly after a short but terrible illness. He told Michael that he couldn't be a father to Walt any more. Michael was angry. He was also surprised at Brian's next words. 'I'm not good at being a father to Walt. There's something about him.'

Brian explained that Walt was different from other children. Strange things happened when he was around. He gave Michael the ticket for the flight and soon after that, Michael arrived in Sydney. He was taking home the son he didn't know …

Now, on the island, Michael realized he still didn't know Walt. He was starting to think that it was the island's fault. If so, they had to get away.

Michael thought about the problem and decided to build a boat. Soon he couldn't think of anything else.

Sayid told him that he had some maps from Danielle's camp. These maps could lead the way to something important on the island, but Michael wasn't interested. 'Walt and I are leaving this place,' he said.

Walt was less interested in leaving the island than his father. He spent a lot of his time with a comic he'd found on the plane. He couldn't read the comic because it was in Spanish, but he loved the pictures.

Michael tried to be friendly, so Walt helped to find things for the boat. Building it wouldn't be easy. But at least they had started.

✈

Everyone seems to have problems with Sawyer. These days he mostly spends his time reading on the beach. Today, Charlie discovered that Sawyer was reading Claire's diary. He went to get the diary from Sawyer. But Sawyer wouldn't give it to him. Instead, he pretended to read bad things she had written about Charlie. Charlie hit him and they started fighting. Kate shouted at them to stop. Charlie took the diary and walked off.

✈

The boat-building is going very slowly. Walt never helps his father for very long. He usually finds an excuse to get away. This time he went to get some drinking water. On the way he found Locke and Boone in the forest. When Locke saw Walt, he told him to go back to his father. A few moments later, Michael appeared and immediately got angry. Locke tried to explain, but Michael wouldn't listen.

Then Walt said something that really hurt Michael. 'Where were you when I was growing up?' he said. 'You never cared. You're not my father.'

Michael was so angry he took Walt's comic and threw it on the fire. 'You *will* listen to me!' shouted Michael and once again, father and son were like strangers.

A little later, Walt took Vincent and went off into the forest. Michael went to look for his son. He went straight to Locke. He thought Walt must be with him. But Locke hadn't seen him. He could see that Michael was really worried. 'Let's go and find your boy,' said Locke.

They found Walt deep in the forest in a circle of trees. He was trying to hide from a hungry polar bear. The bear was about to attack him. Quickly, Michael climbed one of the trees above Walt. He asked Locke to throw a knife to him. He threw the knife down to Walt. 'If it comes near you, use it!' he shouted to his son.

The bear suddenly jumped at Walt. Walt used the knife and managed to hurt the bear. Then Michael jumped down and tied a rope around Walt. Locke held the other end and pulled Walt to safety. Now the bear was attacking Michael. As it came closer, he stuck the knife into its body. The bear cried in pain and went off into the forest. Walt was safe.

Walt threw his arms around Michael's shoulders. They stayed like that for some time. At last Walt realized how much his father loved him.

Back at the beach camp, Michael showed Walt a small wooden box. It came from Walt's house in Sydney. The box was full of Michael's letters to Walt. None of them had been opened. Walt realized his mother had kept them from him. 'She didn't want me to read them,' he said sadly.

'I think she did, one day,' said Michael. 'Because she didn't throw them away.'

✈

Charlie can't stop himself reading Claire's diary. He's very worried. Claire wrote about her dreams in the diary. In one of the dreams, she talks about 'The Black Rock'. The strange Frenchwoman, Danielle, also said something about 'The Black Rock' to Sayid. What is 'The Black Rock'?

✈

It's now evening time and Boone and Locke are in the forest. They are looking for Walt's dog, Vincent. They hear something coming towards them and immediately stand still. Moments later, a person comes out of the trees and stands in front of them. It is Claire! She is shaking and covered in blood and dirt.

She looks afraid – very afraid.

CHAPTER 3 'WE WANT HIM ALIVE'

Jack carried Claire into camp. We are so happy that Claire and her baby are safe, Charlie most of all. But when she sees everyone she starts to scream, 'Who are you? Who are you people?'

Claire can't remember anything about her time on the island. The last thing she remembers is getting on the plane in Sydney. She doesn't know Charlie or anyone else. She's really frightened, but Charlie stays by her side. He gives her the diary. He hopes that it will help her to remember. He hopes that they'll soon be as close as they were before.

The fear of losing Claire makes Charlie remember someone else he lost. Her name was Lucy and her father was very rich. Charlie had met her when his band weren't making money any more. Lucy's father found Charlie a job. But Charlie didn't have

enough money to buy drugs for himself and his 'friends'. A 'friend' called Tommy told Charlie to steal something valuable from Lucy's father. He could then sell it to buy drugs. But the plan went badly wrong. Some friends of Lucy's father found out about it. Charlie told Lucy he was sorry and said he wanted to take care of her. 'You'll never take care of anyone,' she'd said and shut the door in his face.

✈

The next day, Charlie and Jin were walking in the forest when Ethan Rom suddenly attacked them. Ethan was the strange man who had taken Claire away.

Ethan threw a rock at Jin and he fell to the ground unconscious. Then he put his hands round Charlie's neck. 'Bring Claire back to me, here,' he said. 'Or I'll kill one person every day. And you'll be the last.'

When Jack heard about this, he wanted to move everyone to the caves. Locke disagreed. He thought it was better to form a circle of traps around both camps.

A little later, Jack spoke to Kate. She suggested using the guns from the police guard's suitcase. No one else knew about these guns, but maybe the time had come to use them. Jack decided that Locke's plan was best. It was too dangerous to put guns into untrained hands.

✈

The next morning, something made Jack think again. We found one of the survivors with a broken neck on the beach. The dead man's name was Scott Jackson. Ethan had killed him. The circle of traps hadn't worked. Ethan had come in from the sea.

Jack asked Locke if he could find Ethan before he attacked again.

'No chance,' Locke replied. 'He knows the island better than I do. And we have nothing to protect ourselves ...'

At that moment Jack decided to show Locke the guns. He opened the suitcase and Locke picked one up. From the way he held the gun, it was clear he had used one before.

They thought of a new plan. They would take Claire to the place where Ethan had attacked Jin and Charlie. Then a few people with guns would hide until Ethan arrived. It was important not to kill him. They needed information. Who was he? What did he know about the island?

Charlie thought it was too dangerous. But Claire wanted to help. She didn't want anyone else to get hurt.

But who would use the guns? There were four of them in the suitcase. Sayid had been a soldier and he knew more about guns than anyone. So he took the first gun. Jack, as leader, took the second. He gave the third gun to Locke and the fourth to Sawyer. Kate was angry about this. She knew about guns and wanted to go with them. Sawyer understood her feelings. He went to his tent, took out another gun and gave it to her. He had taken it from the police guard on the plane. No one knew that all this time Sawyer had a gun.

✈

As evening came Jack, Sayid, Locke, Sawyer and Kate got ready to leave with Claire.

'Remember,' said Sayid. 'We want him alive.'

They followed Claire to the place in the forest where Ethan had attacked Jin and Charlie.

It was raining hard when they arrived. Claire walked to a space between the trees. The others hid and waited.

For a while, all they could hear was the sound of the rain. Claire stood, lonely and silent, ahead of them.

Suddenly, there was a quick movement in the trees and Ethan appeared. He ran after Claire. Jack jumped onto Ethan and they fought. As Jack jumped, his gun fell onto the forest floor.

Ethan was very strong, but this time Jack was prepared. He hit and kicked Ethan again and again. Sayid and the others stood around pointing their guns at Ethan. This should have been the end. But it wasn't. Suddenly, four shots sounded and blood started pouring from Ethan's chest. Seconds later, he was dead.

Charlie stood over Ethan with a gun in his hand. He was so worried about Claire that he had followed the others through the forest. When he saw Jack's gun on the ground, he couldn't stop himself.

It's night time now at the caves. Jack has come to speak to Charlie. He asks Charlie why he killed Ethan. Charlie looks at Jack in the eyes and says, 'I wasn't going to let that animal near her again – ever!'

CHAPTER 4 SAWYER'S MISTAKE

Jack isn't happy that Sawyer has a gun. He thinks Sawyer could be dangerous. Kate says that she will try to get it from him. But when she goes to see Sawyer, he refuses to give her the gun.

Kate realizes that Sawyer is not as hard as he pretends. He keeps waking in the night after the same bad dream looking lost and uncertain. He has had the nightmare since he was a young boy. His name wasn't Sawyer then. It was James Ford.

James's nightmare is always the same. It begins with the sound of his father banging on the front door. Then his mother comes into his room and tells him to hide under the bed. 'Don't come out, whatever happens,' she says. Then she is gone. Moments later, he hears shouts, the sound of a gun, a body falling. He sees his father's boots from under the bed. They cross the bedroom floor, then stop as his father sits on the bed. The sound of a gun shot fills the room and his father's legs go still.

This is what can happen when a bad man destroys a family. The bad man tricked James's father and stole all his money. The man's name was Frank Sawyer.

He had this nightmare again last night. When he woke up this morning, a huge boar was standing there looking at him. The boar ran off and Sawyer chased it into the forest. As he stood looking for the boar, he heard whispers in the trees. 'Am I going crazy?' he wondered.

Crazy or not, Sawyer wanted to kill the boar. He didn't think it would be difficult. He still had the gun.

Sawyer heard the whispers again. Suddenly, the boar came running out towards him. He only just jumped out of the way in time. A little later Kate appeared and found Sawyer lying on the ground looking angry and afraid. She offered to help Sawyer hunt the boar. 'But first you have to promise something,' she said. 'Give me what I want from the things you've taken from the plane. You also have to give me the gun.' Sawyer agreed but he wasn't very happy about it. They continued the hunt for the boar.

Sawyer remembered the last time he hunted with a gun. That time he was hunting a man, not an animal. A criminal called Hibbs had told him that Frank Sawyer was living in Sydney. Sawyer hated Hibbs, but he hated Frank Sawyer more for destroying his family. He arrived in Australia, bought a gun and went to find Frank. He knew where to look. Hibbs had told him that Frank sold fish down by the ocean.

Sawyer found Frank selling fish from a truck. But the idea of killing a man made him feel sick. He left and went to a bar. There was an older man in the bar. He was an American, too. He told Sawyer that he was once an important doctor in the USA. His son was a doctor, too. They had disagreed about something. As a result, the older man had lost his job.

Now the son thought his father hated him. But this wasn't true.

'Just one phone call,' he said, looking at a phone on the wall. 'And I could tell my son I love him.'

'Why don't you?' Sawyer asked.

'Because I'm too weak,' the man replied.

At that moment, Sawyer thought this was true of him, too. He had been too weak to kill the man who destroyed his family. He put his glass down and went back to Frank's truck.

It was raining when Sawyer shot Frank. As he was dying, Frank asked Sawyer who had sent him. 'Hibbs,' he replied.

Frank told Sawyer that Hibbs had wanted money from him. He had gone to Australia without giving Hibbs the money. So Hibbs had used Sawyer to kill him.

Sawyer felt terrible. He realized he had killed the wrong man. But it was too late to change anything. He felt so bad that he changed his name from James Ford to Sawyer.

A person never feels the same after killing someone. Sawyer isn't the only one to know this. Charlie has discovered it, too. After killing Ethan, he has become very quiet. Hurley was very worried about Charlie. He asked Sayid to speak to him. Sayid was a soldier in Iraq. He knows more than anyone how killing can change you.

Sayid told Charlie that he would never be able to forget taking the life of another. 'But you're not alone,' he said. 'So don't try to be.'

✈

The hunt for the boar has taken Kate and Sawyer far from camp. They decide to spend the night in the forest.

The next morning, Sawyer wakes up and finds his

things are destroyed. He knows immediately what has happened. The boar visited them in the night. But it only attacked his things. 'It really wants to get me,' he thinks.

At that moment Locke finds them. He tells Sawyer a story about a strange dog. It appeared one day at his mother's house after his sister had died in an accident. The mother thought the accident was her fault. The dog stayed with his mother for many years. His mother thought that the dog was Locke's sister. She had come to forgive her for the accident. After Locke's mother died, the dog disappeared. No one knew where it had come from or where it went.

Sawyer thinks about the story. Does the boar really want to get him? Maybe it has come to forgive him.

✈

Kate and Sawyer continue their hunt and soon they find the boar. It is standing very still under a tree. Sawyer lifts his gun and points it at the boar's head. Kate waits for the shot. But no shot comes.

Sawyer lets the gun drop to his side. 'It's just a boar,' he says. 'Let's go back to camp.'

CHAPTER 5 FIRE ON THE BEACH

Sun was walking along the beach in a bikini this morning. Most people wouldn't see anything wrong with that. But her husband Jin did. He picked up a towel and threw it around her shoulders. He was upset that his wife was showing her body to other people. He took Sun's hand and started pulling her up the beach.

Michael thought that Jin was attacking her. He ran to Sun to protect her. But when Michael shouted at Jin, Sun hit him. Michael was surprised and upset.

Jin walked off and Sun told Michael she was sorry.

'It's your problem,' Michael said and walked away.

As he walked up the beach he saw his boat and he started to feel better. It was really beginning to look like a boat now. Everyone was talking about it. Sawyer had even booked himself a ticket.

✈

Sadly, Michael's dream of escape might now be over. Jin was the first to see the boat burning. He ran over and tried to put out the fire. But the fire was too strong and he burnt his arms.

Jin left the beach and sat alone at the edge of the forest. He wondered about Sun and Michael. Yes, Sun had hit Michael, but he feared they were becoming too friendly.

Jin thought of all the trouble he had taken to make Sun his wife. First he had lied about his family. His father was a poor fisherman and he didn't want Sun's father, Mr Paik, to meet him. So he told Paik that his father was dead. Mr Paik had agreed to the marriage, but there was a price to pay. Jin had to work for him.

He soon discovered that Paik was a hard, dishonest businessman. He was also very dangerous. Mr Han, a government officer, wrote a bad report about one of Paik's factories. So he sent Jin to Han's house to tell him to change the report. Han said sorry, but the report wasn't changed. Paik was angry with Jin. He told him to go back to the house with another man. This time there would be no mistake. Jin knew what this meant. The other man was going to kill Han. Jin knew he couldn't let this happen, so he got to the house first. When Han answered the door, Jin pushed him back into the house and started hitting him. Han's wife and daughter were screaming but Jin didn't stop. Before he left, he looked at Han and whispered, 'I just saved your life.'

After this, Jin went to see his father, the fisherman. He told him everything. His father wasn't angry. He just told Jin to finish the present job he was doing for Mr Paik. Then he must leave. Jin promised his father he would do this.

Back at the beach, the boat is now a pile of burnt wood and black metal. Michael thinks that Jin started the fire that burnt the boat. Sawyer thinks so, too. They go to find Jin.

Sawyer reaches Jin first. He pulls him down to the beach. Everyone sees the burn marks on Jin's arms. Jack says this doesn't mean that Jin started the fire. But Michael doesn't listen. He hits Jin and knocks him down. Jack wants to stop the fight but Sayid and Sawyer say it's a fair fight between two men. Jack moves back. People form a circle around Jin and Michael. Jin gets up from the sand. He doesn't fight back, but he's not frightened either. Every time Michael knocks him down, he gets up again and shouts at him in Korean. Suddenly Sun screams in English, 'Leave him alone!'

Everyone stands still. Most people don't know that Sun can speak English. No one is more surprised or upset than Jin. He gives Sun a horrible look and walks from the beach, alone.

Locke saw what happened as he returned from the forest. He tells everyone that it is stupid to fight. 'Our real enemies are out there,' he says, pointing to the forest. 'We're not the only people on the island and you know it.'

Later that evening, Locke is playing a board game with Walt. Suddenly he asks, 'Why did you burn the boat?' Walt is silent for a moment. 'I don't want to leave the island,' he says. 'I like it here.'

Locke smiles. 'I like it here, too,' he says.

CHAPTER 6 A PROBLEM WITH NUMBERS

Everyone likes Hurley. He's friendly, generous and good company. But even he has secrets in his past. Hurley's secrets aren't about people. They're about numbers. No one would guess that he won $156 million in the USA. And no one would guess that he's frightened by the winning numbers.

He didn't expect to see the numbers on the island. But he was wrong.

It happened this morning. He was helping Michael and Jin with the boat. Michael wants Sayid to build a radar for the boat. The radar will need a large battery. Everyone knows that Danielle, the Frenchwoman, has batteries. They need to find Danielle.

Sayid said that finding Danielle was a crazy idea. He waved the maps and papers he'd taken from her camp. 'The area where she lives is very dangerous,' he said. 'You might never come back.'

Hurley went very quiet. He looked at one of Danielle's papers and saw the numbers. The numbers were: 4 8 15 16 23 42. They were repeated many times. These were exactly the same numbers Hurley had used to win the $156 million. A few seconds later, he gave the maps and papers back to Sayid. But he secretly kept the paper with the numbers.

Hurley thought back to the night he won the money. He was eating and watching the TV. His mother was telling him he ate too much. He should go out more and find a nice girl. Hurley wasn't listening. A woman on the TV was reading out the winning numbers: 4 8 15 16 23 42.

Hurley pulled out his ticket. They were the numbers he had

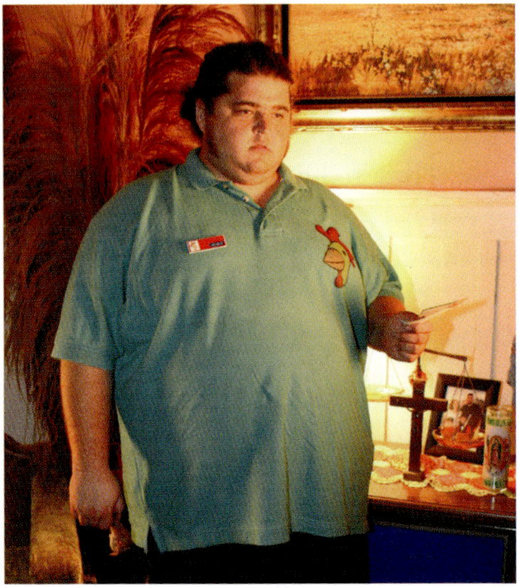

chosen. He had won a huge amount of money. The surprise was too much and he fell unconscious on the floor.

Everything has its bad side. Hurley soon realized this when news reporters were talking to him and his family outside his house. His grandfather, Tito, suddenly dropped dead of a heart attack. Later, his mother broke her foot. She was getting out of Hurley's car to look at the new house he had bought for her. When they both looked up, they saw that the house was on fire. In less than a minute, the police arrived. They thought Hurley had started the fire so they took him away.

The police soon let him go. They also had to pay him because he hadn't done anything wrong. Now he had even more money. And it kept growing. His business interests were very successful for him, but bad luck for others. A storm in Florida destroyed fields of oranges. A factory caught fire and eight people died. In both cases, Hurley was covered and he made even more money. He began to think that the winning numbers were bringing bad luck to everyone except him.

Hurley wanted to find out about the numbers so much that he didn't take Sayid's advice. He knew he had to find Danielle and ask her about them. He tried to leave the camp immediately, but met Charlie on the way into the forest. Hurley was in such a hurry to get away that Charlie felt worried about him. Charlie told Jack and Sayid and they decided to follow Hurley.

They reached him at a dangerous moment. Hurley had stepped on one of Danielle's traps. 'Don't move!' shouted Sayid. Hurley looked up. There was a huge ball of sharp sticks hanging just above his head. But Hurley wasn't worried. With the numbers, he knew he was a lucky man. He jumped to one side. Charlie, Jack and Sayid closed their eyes. The ball of sticks just missed Hurley and crashed to the ground.

Hurley thought back to where he got the numbers. He remembered a crazy man called Lenny. Hurley had met Lenny in a psychiatric hospital when they were both patients. Lenny used to repeat the same numbers 4 8 15 16 23 42 over and over again. When all the bad things started happening to people around him, Hurley decided to find out more about the numbers.

He went back to the hospital where Lenny was still a patient. Hurley asked Lenny about the numbers, but he just sat there quietly repeating them over and over again. Hurley then told Lenny that he had used the numbers to win the money. Lenny suddenly stopped. 'You shouldn't have done that!' he screamed at Hurley. 'You've opened the box! You've got to get away from the numbers!'

Nurses came and took Lenny away. As they were pulling him from the room, Hurley asked Lenny who he got the numbers from. Lenny cried out a name: 'Sam Tooney in Australia.'

Hurley went to Australia to find Tooney. He found his house but was too late. Tooney's wife told him that her husband had died four years earlier. But she agreed to tell Hurley more about the numbers.

Sixteen years ago, her husband and Lenny had worked together on a lonely island in the Pacific. Their job was to listen out for radio messages for the US government. The job was mostly boring. But one night, they heard the numbers repeated on the radio over and over again. Many years later, Tooney used the numbers at a fair and won a lot of money. On the way home, their car crashed. Tooney was unhurt but his wife lost her leg. Many bad things happened after that. In the end, Tooney killed himself. He thought it was the only way to stop the bad things happening.

Tooney's wife, like everyone else, didn't believe the numbers were bad. Hurley was unhappy. If she didn't believe him, who would?

The four men continued on through the forest towards Danielle's camp. After some time they came to a rope bridge across a deep valley. The bridge looked very unsafe and there was a huge drop below. Hurley wasn't afraid, but the others didn't want him to cross. He didn't listen and crossed the bridge easily. Charlie crossed next. The bridge broke just as he managed to get to the other side. Jack and Sayid were left behind. They agreed to meet Hurley and Charlie at Danielle's camp.

In the end, Jack and Sayid were the first to find the camp. As they got closer, they stepped into a more dangerous trap. Suddenly, there were several loud explosions. Luckily they were unhurt, but Danielle's camp was destroyed. They looked at what was left. There was nothing except part of the photo of Sayid's friend, Nadia. He had left it behind when he last visited Danielle's camp. One thing was clear. Danielle knew they were coming.

As they made their way through the forest, Charlie asked Hurley why he was acting so strangely. Hurley was about to tell him about the numbers when suddenly a gun fired at them. Charlie ran off into the forest, but Hurley just stood there with the paper in his hands. Danielle came out of the trees and pointed the gun in his face. He wasn't afraid. He held up the paper with the numbers. 'What do they mean?' he asked Danielle.

Danielle realized that Hurley wasn't dangerous and lowered the gun. She told him that she first heard the numbers on a radio out in the Pacific. She was on a boat with a group of scientists. Soon after that, their boat crashed on the rocks near the island and they swam to safety. Some time later, they found out where the radio message had come from. It came from near 'The Black Rock'. For Danielle, the numbers had brought bad luck, too. All the group of scientists, except her, had later died of a strange illness.

Hurley suddenly smiled. Finally he had found someone who believed the numbers were bad. 'Thank you,' he said and put his arms around Danielle.

✈

Charlie finally found Jack and Sayid near Danielle's old camp. They were looking for Hurley when he suddenly appeared in front of them. He looked at them calmly, smiled, and gave them a large battery. 'This is from Danielle,' he said. 'She says "Hi!"'

✈

It's now evening and Hurley and Charlie are sitting by the campfire. Charlie asks Hurley why he was acting so strangely. 'I think that the plane crash was my fault,' Hurley answers. 'And all the bad stuff that's happening.'

Charlie laughs at this. He tells Hurley that he's not the only one with bad things in his life. He tells him about his drug problem. Now he wants Hurley to be honest. What is *his* big secret? He tells Charlie that back home, he is worth $156 million.

Charlie is angry. He has been honest and all he gets in return is a joke. He walks off, leaving Hurley alone.

✈

Deep in the forest, Locke and Boone are studying a line of numbers on the hatch. The numbers are: 4 8 15 16 23 42.

CHAPTER 7 A TERRIBLE ACCIDENT

Of all the survivors John Locke is probably the most happy to be here. He believes that the island has given him a wonderful gift – after the crash he was able to stand up and walk again. And since that day, his understanding of the island has grown and grown. But right now, Locke is feeling a lot less confident about everything.

One of the reasons is the hatch. He felt so sure that the island would show him how to open it. But everything he and Boone tried was unsuccessful. They were getting nowhere. And now Locke is wondering if his belief in the island is leaving him. Even worse, could the island be losing its belief in him?

The next day Locke felt much better. A sign had come to him in the night. He had dreamt of a plane crashing in the forest. It wasn't the plane the survivors had been on. It was a small plane and for some reason it was very important.

He told Boone about the dream. Locke wanted to go and find the plane straight away. Boone wasn't optimistic. He didn't think the plane was real.

They walked for a long time through the forest without finding anything. But then they saw something hanging in a tree. They looked closer and saw that it was the dead body of a man. Then they found some Nigerian money and a gun. But as they moved on, Locke's legs began to stop working. 'Is the island taking away the gift it has given me?' he wondered.

Locke thought about his past. He thought about what happened to him before he had to use a wheelchair. It began with a mystery woman. He saw her one day in the shop where he was working. She was looking at him in a strange way. He saw her again later in a car park. She tried to run away but he caught her. They went for a coffee and she told him that her name was Emily Locke. Emily was the mother he never knew. When John Locke was a baby, she gave him away. She told him he was 'special' but she didn't explain why.

Locke asked a private detective to find out more. The detective told him that Emily was a psychiatric patient. She had been unable to care for a baby, so she gave him away.

'What about my father?' Locke asked.

The detective knew who his father was, but he didn't want to tell Locke. 'Do you really want to know?' he asked. 'It will only end unhappily.'

Locke wanted the information. He found that his father was a rich man called Anthony Cooper. Locke found out where he lived and went to see him. Cooper seemed happy that his son had found him. Soon they became very close.

One day, Locke arrived at Cooper's house early. He found Cooper sitting beside a kidney machine. He told Locke that he needed a new kidney. It was unlikely that he would get one. Hospitals gave them to young people first. Straight away Locke offered him one of his own kidneys. It seemed a natural part of the happy story between father and son.

But it wasn't. When Locke came out of hospital, Cooper didn't want to see him any more. Locke had been tricked.

Locke's legs were now almost useless and Boone had to help him walk. Just when they were about to give up the search, Locke saw the plane. It was stuck high up in a huge tree. Locke couldn't walk any further so Boone climbed up the tree alone. He got into the plane and looked around. Inside he found a map of Nigeria and many plastic bags full of drugs. He also found a radio – and it was working. Boone immediately began sending a message for help.

He never finished his message. The plane fell from the tree and crashed to the forest floor. Locke watched, feeling terrible. He saw Boone's body covered in blood. At that moment, all the feeling came back into his legs. He picked up the unconscious Boone and put him on his back. Then he began the long journey to camp.

✈

Back at the beach Sawyer thinks he might be dying of a dangerous illness. He has had a lot of bad headaches over the last few days. He asks for Jack's advice. It doesn't take Jack long to discover the problem. Sawyer needs glasses for reading. He is so happy that the problem isn't serious that he and Jack start laughing.

The laughing stops when Locke appears carrying Boone. It is clear to Jack that Boone is very badly injured. Locke explains that Boone fell off a rock. Then he disappears back into the forest.

'Locke!' Jack shouts. But he's gone.

Jack calls Sun. They have to act quickly to save Boone's life.

✈

Deep in the forest, Locke is now sitting next to the hatch. 'I've done everything you've asked!' he shouts.

As if in answer, a light suddenly shines through the small window in the hatch.

CHAPTER 8 LETTING GO

Jack and Sun will do everything they can to save Boone. It won't be easy. Boone has lost a lot of blood, his right leg is badly broken and he can hardly breathe. Jack makes a hole in his chest and Boone's breathing becomes easier. He tells Kate to get all the medicine she can from Sawyer.

'Boone, listen,' says Jack. 'You are not going to die.'

On her way back with the medicine, Kate heard a noise in the forest. She stopped and looked around. Moments later, a woman came out of the forest holding her stomach. It was Claire. She was about to have her baby.

'Help!' she shouted. Jin heard Claire and came running to join them.

'Get Jack,' Kate told him. It didn't matter that Jin spoke no English. He understood immediately what to do.

Jin raced through the forest to the camp at the caves. He could see that Jack was busy giving his own blood to Boone through a plastic pipe. Sun was acting as his nurse. They certainly weren't going to leave their patient. Through Sun, Jack explained that Kate would have to manage the birth. When Charlie appeared, Jack told him to go and help Claire. He told him what they needed to do.

✈

Jack and Sun tried and tried to help Boone. At one point, Boone began to speak. Jack thought he heard him talk about falling and a plane. He didn't understand. Locke had told him that Boone had fallen from a large rock.

Then Boone whispered something. 'It's because of the hatch,' he said. 'Locke told me not to tell anyone.'

The hatch? Jack wondered what Boone was talking about. Whatever it was, he knew that Locke had been lying. Boone hadn't just fallen. Something heavy had fallen on him. Locke was hiding something. This made Jack very angry. Locke had left them with no information about what happened. No information to save Boone's life. But Jack made a promise – he wasn't going to let Boone die.

Jack remembered making a similar promise to his wife, Sarah. Sarah had been his patient. He had saved her life after a terrible car crash. Just before their wedding, he wondered if he was marrying her because of this promise. He even talked about this fear to his father.

'The problem with you, Jack, is that you just can't let go,' his father had replied.

At the wedding Jack realized that he truly loved Sarah and wanted to marry her. But he also realized that his father was right. He did find it hard to let go …

Jack did not want to let Boone go. He would do anything to save him. He even wanted to cut off his leg using the metal door of the plane.

'You can't save him, Jack,' Michael cried.

Jack was very angry. 'This is our best chance!' he cried.

'I know you made a promise,' said Boone. 'But you can't keep it, Jack. Just let me go.' Jack realized that Boone was about to die. There was nothing more he could do. 'I'm sorry,' Jack said, fighting back the tears.

Later that night, Claire gave birth to a healthy baby. The next morning she carried the little boy proudly in her arms. Everyone crowded around to look at him. One life had left us. A new life had arrived.

Shannon and Sayid had spent the night together on a different beach. They didn't know yet about Boone. As they walked back to the camp, Shannon saw the crowd of people around Claire. Jack left the crowd. He had to tell her the terrible news about her brother. Shannon looked at Jack with disbelief. Suddenly she felt completely alone in the world.

Jack told Sayid about the things Boone said before he died, about the plane and the hatch. He wondered if Sayid knew anything. Sayid shook his head. He knew nothing about them.

Kate is sitting with Jack on the beach. She wants to know how he feels about Boone's death.

'Boone didn't just die,' said Jack angrily. 'He was murdered. And I'm going to find the man who did it!'

CHAPTER 9 QUESTIONS AND LIES

Kate was worried about Jack. She knew Jack hadn't slept, he'd given blood and he'd lost a patient. And now he was out in the forest searching for Locke. She decided to go and find him.

It didn't take her long. Jack was too weak to go very far. He wanted to continue the search. But after a few uncertain steps, he realized it was useless. He let Kate help him back to camp.

✈

A little later that day, we all formed a circle around Boone's body. Shannon was too upset to say anything.

Sayid spoke instead. 'I didn't know Boone very well,' he said. 'But I know that on our sixth day here a woman – Joanna – died in the ocean. Boone was the first to try to save her. He was a brave man … He will be missed.'

Suddenly, we heard a voice behind us. 'It was my fault.' Everyone turned around and saw John Locke.

Locke knew he had to explain. He told us about the plane. He couldn't go into it himself because his leg was injured. Boone went instead. He found a radio. He was sending a message when the plane fell. It happened because he was trying to help.

Jack didn't believe him. 'Where were you?' he shouted angrily over and over again. He walked up to Locke and pushed him to the ground. When he grabbed Locke's neck, Sawyer had to pull him away. Moments later, Jack fell down. He was too tired and weak to stand up any more.

Kate took Jack back to camp and made him a drink. He wanted to go after Locke again. But this time he couldn't. Kate had put something in the drink to make him sleep.

Locke went to speak to Shannon. He told her he was sorry about what happened to Boone. Shannon listened but she didn't say anything.

After Locke had left, Shannon went to see Sayid. 'You asked me once if you could do anything for me,' she said.

'Anything,' Sayid replied.

'Locke killed my brother. Will you do something about that?' Shannon's question put Sayid in a difficult position. He wanted to help, but he wasn't sure that Boone's death was really Locke's fault.

Sayid wasn't a stranger to problems like this. Before he took the plane from Sydney, he discovered that Nadia was alive. A woman from the CIA told him this after they caught him in Australia. The woman offered to let Sayid go. She would also give him Nadia's address. But first he had to do something for the CIA. He had to find some explosives stolen by a group of terrorists. The CIA knew that one of the terrorists was an old school friend of Sayid's. His name was Essam Tazir. Unhappily, Sayid agreed to help them.*

Sayid found Essam and managed to join his terrorist group. The group wanted Essam to wear explosives and attack a government building. He would die in the attack. Essam agreed. He was angry. His wife had died in the Iraq war and his life was empty without her. But he didn't want to kill ordinary people. He told Sayid about his fears. Sayid told him not to do it. He explained that he was working for the CIA. Essam couldn't understand how his old friend could work for the enemy. He was so upset that he shot himself.

Sayid had done what the CIA wanted and they gave him Nadia's address. But he had also lost a dear friend.

Sayid wanted to discover the truth about Boone's death. He found Locke and told him he wanted to get the radio

* The CIA works for the US government. It tries to get secret information from foreign countries.

from the small plane. Locke agreed to show him where it was. As they walked through the forest Sayid started to ask questions.

'Why did you lie about the plane?'

Locke said that was a mistake.

'If you had a leg injury, how could you carry Boone back to camp?' Sayid asked.

'Because getting Boone back to camp was more important than my leg,' Locke replied.

Sayid noticed a gun in Locke's trouser pocket. When he asked about it, Locke said it came from the body of one of the plane's passengers. He gave the gun to Sayid. 'Now do you believe me?' he asked.

Sayid just gave Locke a hard look. Locke knew Sayid needed something more …

'Do you remember about a week after the crash someone knocked you unconscious?' Locke asked.

'You mean when I was trying to find where the radio message was coming from?' Sayid remembered Danielle's radio message asking for help. For sixteen years it had played over and over again. Sayid wanted to discover where the message was coming from. But just before he found the answer, someone hit him and destroyed his equipment.

'Yes,' said Locke. 'I lied to you. Sawyer didn't hit you. It was me.'

Sayid was so angry that he took the gun and held it against Locke's neck. Locke said he had done it to protect everyone. Did Sayid really want to take everyone to the place where something had killed all of Danielle's people? Everyone wanted to leave the island so much, no one was thinking clearly at that time.

Sayid put the gun down. He still thought Locke was

keeping secrets. But now he didn't think that Boone's death was Locke's fault.

✈

Sayid went to speak to Shannon. He didn't know why Locke had lied about the plane, but Boone's death had been a terrible accident. Shannon was angry. 'Just forget about it, OK,' she said and walked off.

✈

Jack woke up some time later from a deep sleep. As he came round he felt for the key to the suitcase. It wasn't there. Someone must have taken it to get the guns. Immediately Jack thought it must be Locke. He set off into the forest to look for him.

When Sayid found out that someone had taken the guns, he realized it wasn't Locke ... it was Shannon! He chased after Jack and told him his fears.

When they found Locke, Shannon was pointing a gun at his head. Sayid managed to knock her down as the gun went off. He had saved Locke's life. But had he lost Shannon?

'Get away from me!' she screamed at him.

✈

Back at camp, Locke thanked Sayid for saving his life.

'I did it because you will help us survive,' Sayid replied. 'Now, take me to the hatch.'

'What hatch?' Locke answered.

Sayid gave him a long, hard look.

'Please, John,' he said. 'No more lies.'

CHAPTER 10 BAD WATER

Michael has put a lot of care into building his boat. It's almost ready to go, but he wants to spend more time on it. He wants it to be just right. But this morning Dr Arzt, a science teacher, told him to leave immediately. Arzt explained that the monsoon* season was coming. Very soon the winds would change. The boat would go south into cold Antarctic waters, not north where they could be rescued.

Michael thought about this and decided that they had no choice. They would leave tomorrow.

* The monsoon season is a time of strong winds and heavy rain in South East Asia.

Kate is really worried about this news. When Michael brings the rescuers to the island, the police will catch her. If she goes on the boat, she will at least have the chance to escape. She has to speak to Michael.

'Have you got enough food and water for the journey?' Kate asks him.

Michael is surprised. 'Why are you suddenly interested?'

'Because I'm going with you,' she answers.

Michael explains that the boat can only take four people. These are Walt, himself, Jin and Sawyer. Kate tells him that Sawyer will be trouble. She should take his place. Michael says no. Sawyer has given him a lot of things for the boat. In return, Michael has agreed to take him with them. He has made a promise.

✈

Kate thought of a way to escape from the police. She would pretend to be someone else. She found a passport from one of the plane's passengers. It was Joanna's, the woman who had died in the ocean. Kate burnt Joanna's photo and put her own in the passport instead. Sawyer caught Kate doing this. He knew that Kate was trying to take his place in the boat. He also knew her secret – back in the USA she was a wanted criminal.

'If you try to take my place on the boat,' Sawyer told Kate, 'I'll tell Michael the truth about you. Michael won't want a criminal on his boat.'

'If I want your place, Sawyer, I'll get it,' said Kate and she walked off.

✈

In another part of the island, Sayid was leading Jack deep into the forest. Jack had no idea where they were going. He was about to tell Sayid to take him back when they arrived at the hatch. Locke was waiting for them. Jack was angry with Locke. Why had he kept the hatch a secret? Locke replied that Jack had kept his secrets, too. He hadn't told the others about the suitcase with the guns inside. Jack couldn't disagree. He looked more closely at the hatch. 'How do we get inside this thing?' he asked.

Sayid explained why they couldn't open it. It wasn't meant to be opened. There was no hole for a key and nothing to hold onto to pull it open. There must be something very dangerous inside.

Jack and Locke still wanted to get inside. They thought that the hatch would be important for their survival. They would have to think of a way to open it. They were on their way back to the camp when Kate ran up to them.

'It's Michael,' she said. 'He's sick.'

They all raced back to the beach camp. Jack found Michael lying on the beach.

Jack asked him some questions and soon he knew what was wrong. Building the boat was hot work. They kept bottles of water near them at all times. Someone had put something into his drinking water to make him ill. Michael thought it was Sawyer. He thought he had done it so Kate could take his place on the boat. He knew Sawyer found Kate attractive.

When Sawyer heard about this, he was very angry. He told everyone Kate's secret. 'This woman is a criminal. She was the police guard's prisoner on the plane!' he cried. 'And I saw her changing Joanna's passport. She wanted to use it as her own.'

Kate was in big trouble now. Everyone thought that she had made Michael sick.

Kate said that Sawyer was right. She was a criminal, but she didn't put anything into Michael's water bottle.

Sawyer's place on the boat was safe again. But he didn't feel good about what he'd done to Kate.

The truth about Kate's past wasn't so simple. Kate remembered going home to see her dying mother at a hospital in Iowa. She was hiding from the police at the time. There were police everywhere looking for her – even at the hospital. Her old boyfriend, Tom, was a doctor at the hospital. Tom's wife and young son were away and he agreed to help her.

Kate and Tom went to a place which was very special to them when they were teenagers. It was below a large tree. In the ground was a box. Many years before, Kate and Tom had put some of their favourite things inside this box. These included the toy plane that Kate later found inside the police guard's suitcase. As they looked at the things, they remembered their young love. Kate and Tom kissed. Then they drove back to the hospital so Kate could see her mother.

But when Kate's mother woke up and saw her daughter, she screamed. The police ran into the room. Tom told her not to run away, but Kate didn't listen. They both ran to Tom's car. Kate started driving away. A policeman shot at the car. He missed Kate but he killed Tom. Kate escaped but she felt terrible. She had killed the man she loved.

Jack thought carefully about who made Michael sick. He found Sun and asked her if she wanted to stop her husband, Jin, leaving the island.

'Did you put something in his water?' he asked. 'Did Michael drink Jin's water by mistake?'

Sun told Jack that he was right. 'I don't want him to die out there,' she said fighting back the tears.

Jack promised not to tell anyone. But he still doesn't know the whole story.

Kate knew about Sun's fears. She suggested to Sun that she should make her husband sick. And now Sun is worried that Kate will get into trouble. 'You were only trying to help me,' she says to Kate later that evening.

'Don't worry,' Kate says. 'Jack's good at keeping secrets.'

CHAPTER 11 DANIELLE RETURNS

Walt is very frightened. Locke has shown him the hatch. Straight away Walt told Locke not to open it. Locke doesn't understand why Walt is so worried. Locke is certain that the hatch is the only hope for our survival.

✈

Walt was even more worried when he woke up this morning. He saw a stranger exploring the beach camp and screamed for his father. Michael woke up. He saw the strange woman and began shouting, too. Soon everyone was awake and stood in a circle around the woman.

Sayid told everyone to stay calm. He knew who she was. It was Danielle, the Frenchwoman who lived alone in the middle of the island.

Danielle wasn't frightened. She seemed more interested in Claire's baby than anything else. As everyone got closer, she told the story of how she had landed on the island sixteen years ago. At the time, she was expecting a baby. All the other people in her group had died of a terrible illness before her baby was born. She had to manage the birth herself. She had called the baby Alex.

A week after the birth, she saw black smoke rising into the air from the middle of the island. It was a bad sign. That night, 'The Others' came and took her baby. 'And now,' she said. 'They'll come for you. You have only three choices: run, hide – or die.'

Jack thought Danielle was crazy. He said this to Locke as they left the beach.

But Locke wasn't so sure.

✈

Danielle's story really frightened everyone. Now it was even more important for the boat to leave immediately. But Michael knew there was a problem.

'It will take too long to get the boat in the water,' Michael explained to Jack. 'We need to find something to push it along.'

Jack got everyone to help. They put pieces of wood in a line from the front of the boat to the sea. When all the pieces of wood were in place, Michael gave the order. 'One, two, three, lift! … Now push!' he shouted.

But it wasn't Michael's lucky day. Half-way to the sea, the boat came off the wood and part of it broke. Now they would have to mend it.

Michael said that it was Sawyer's fault. He hadn't followed his instructions. Sawyer didn't have time to get angry. 'Look!' shouted Walt. He was pointing towards the middle of the island. A line of thick, black smoke was rising into the air.

Was Danielle telling the truth? Did this mean that 'The Others' were coming to get them? 'Run, hide or die', Danielle had said. Jack decided that 'hide' was the best choice. And the best place to hide was inside the hatch.

✈

Locke took Jack, Sayid, Hurley and Danielle to the hatch. Danielle said she had never seen it before. Sayid still didn't want to open it, but the others disagreed. They tried to think of a way to get inside. Suddenly, Locke remembered about the explosives that Danielle had used to destroy her camp. 'Where did you get them from?' he asked her.

'From "The Black Rock",' Daniel replied. She added that 'The Others' always came at night. So they would have to go to 'The Black Rock' and return before dark.

✈

Back at the beach, Jack told the other survivors about their plan. Dr Arzt, the science teacher, told Jack that he wanted to go with them. He knew about explosives. So the group going to 'The Black Rock' would now be Jack, Locke, Kate, Danielle, Hurley and Dr Arzt. Sayid couldn't go because he had to finish the radar for Michael's boat.

✈

Before the group set off, Jack went to find Sawyer. He found him a little way into the forest. He was working hard cutting wood to mend the boat. Jack gave him one of the guns from the suitcase. He was the only one on the boat who could use a gun. Jack thought he might need it for the journey.

For once, Sawyer was grateful. He asked what Jack was going to do with the other guns. Jack told him he would give them to Sayid.

As Jack turned to go, Sawyer realized that they might not see each other again. He wanted to tell Jack about his father. Sawyer told him that he met an American man in a bar in Sydney. The man was a doctor and his son was, too. The man was drinking heavily. He felt bad about what had happened between him and his son. The man had wanted to phone his son and tell him he loved him. 'But I guess he didn't make that phone call, huh?' said Sawyer.

Jack shook his head. He felt very sad, but also grateful to Sawyer. Now he knew that his father had forgiven him.

✈

Just before they left for 'The Black Rock,' Jack and his group came to the beach to say goodbye to Michael, Walt and Jin.

Very soon after Jack and the others had left, Sayid finished the radar and gave it to Michael. The radar could show any ship within forty kilometres of the boat. He also gave Michael a special gun. It could shoot a rocket into the sky at night to get help. 'There's only one rocket,' Sayid explained. 'Be careful about when you use it.'

Walt knew that Shannon was still feeling very sad about Boone. He decided to give her his dog, Vincent. 'He took care of me when my mom died,' Walt said. 'He'll protect you, too.' Shannon was very grateful. Walt really loved his dog.

The saddest goodbye was between Sun and Jin. Sun gave Jin a book she had made. In it she had written some things in English and Korean. It would be useful for the journey. Jin kissed her and told her he was leaving to save her. 'I love you,' Sun replied.

✈

Jack's group are having a difficult journey to 'The Black Rock'. Dr Arzt is frightened by Danielle's stories of 'The Others'. He suddenly decides to go back to camp.

Just after Arzt leaves, they hear the sound of the huge thing coming towards them. Suddenly, Arzt runs back through the trees screaming for help. They all hide in the trees. The sound becomes louder. And then it slowly goes away.

They continue their journey, but they are all really frightened now.

Danielle leads the way. A few minutes later, she stops. 'This is "The Black Rock",' she says.

Jack and the others look to where she is pointing. It is a huge old wooden ship. And the name in big letters on the ship is 'The Black Rock'.

At last, Michael's boat is safely in the sea. A small crowd watches from the beach as Michael, Walt, Sawyer and Jin wave goodbye. They are leaving behind the island and its problems.

Behind them, the line of black smoke is rising in the air.

CHAPTER 12 SAILING AWAY

Why didn't Danielle tell anyone that 'The Black Rock' is a ship? And how did it land in the middle of the forest? Dr Arzt gives the most sensible answer to this question. He says a tsunami* probably moved it there. While the group discuss this, Danielle sets off back into the forest. Jack calls after her, but Locke tells him to let her go. They don't need her any more.

Time is passing. They need to get the explosives quickly. Hurley and Arzt are too frightened to go inside. So Jack tells them to wait outside. Then he goes with Kate and Locke to explore the ship.

* A tsunami is a huge dangerous wave.

It is dark inside 'The Black Rock'. As they walk through the main part of the ship, they hear the sound of metal moving. Locke shines a light. Long black chains hang down from the roof. At the end of the chains are the bodies of dead people.

'Slaves,' Locke whispers. It is clear now that 'The Black Rock' was a slave ship.

They find the explosives in a large wooden box at the back of the ship. Jack and Locke carry the box outside.

'Stop!' Arzt shouts when he sees them. 'Put it down – carefully.'

Jack and Locke put the box slowly onto the ground. Arzt tells them to move away. He opens the box and takes out one of the explosives. He starts to tell the others how dangerous it is in the warm, wet air …

Suddenly, there is a loud explosion and Arzt is killed immediately.

✈

Back at the beach, something terrible has happened, too. Charlie was with Claire and the baby when Danielle came to them. She told them that she needed Sayid. It was very important. Charlie ran off to find Sayid, but Danielle had tricked them.

Moments later, Sayid and Charlie heard

Claire's screams. They ran to her, but it was too late. Danielle had attacked her and taken the baby.

Sayid knows what Danielle is planning. She is going to take Claire's baby to 'The Others'. She wants to give Claire's baby to them hoping that they will return Alex. There is no time to lose. Sayid takes two guns from the suitcase and they race after Danielle.

✈

Following Arzt's terrible accident, Jack and Locke agree that only two people should carry the explosives. They put the explosives carefully into bags. But who will carry them?

Locke picks up four sticks. The two people who pull the shortest sticks from his hand will carry the explosives. Locke and Kate pull the shortest sticks so they must carry the bags.

Jack isn't happy about this. Later, when Kate isn't looking, he changes her bag and carries the explosives himself.

The group makes its way slowly back to the hatch.

Suddenly, they hear the sound of the huge thing. It is coming towards them through the forest. Jack, Kate and Hurley run, but Locke just stands there and waits for it. Jack shouts at him, telling him to run. Locke looks up in wonder at it but then his face shows his fear. Suddenly, he is knocked down, then something pulls him along the ground. Jack runs after him, but he is moving fast.

Moments later, Locke is pulled into a very deep hole. Jack manages to hold onto his arms. Locke shouts to Jack to let him go. But Jack doesn't listen. He tells Kate to throw some of the explosives down the hole.

At first she looks in her own bag, but then Jack tells her to look in his. She takes out one of the explosives and throws it into the hole. There is an explosion deep under the ground. Jack and Kate pull Locke out of the hole.

✈

Michael is already having problems at sea. The boat hit something in the water and the rudder has come off.

Michael feels useless as he watches it disappear under the waves. They cannot control the boat without it.

Suddenly, Sawyer jumps bravely into the water. He manages to get the rudder and pull it back to the boat.

'You just saved us, man,' Michael says.

✈

Charlie can't run as fast as Sayid. This is slowing them down in their hunt for Danielle and the baby. They reach the small plane that Locke and Boone found in the forest. Sayid tells Charlie to rest a little.

Charlie suddenly notices some things on the ground. They are little bags of drugs from the plane. When Sayid isn't looking, he takes one and puts it in his pocket.

After a short rest, they start off again. But not for long. They walk into one of Danielle's traps. A bag of rocks falls on Charlie and his head is badly cut. Sayid stops the blood with an old soldier's trick. He puts some explosive from one of the guns onto Charlie's injury. Then he lights it. It burns Charlie's skin, but it stops the blood.

When they reach the black smoke, night has arrived. There is no sign of 'The Others' Danielle talked about. Perhaps Danielle started the fire herself? As if answering the question, she suddenly appears. She is crying and carrying Claire's baby. 'They're not here,' she says.

Charlie is very angry. He takes the baby back and returns quickly to the beach.

When Claire sees the baby, she is very grateful. Her smile shows that Charlie *can* look after someone he loves.

Shannon is happy, too. Charlie couldn't have saved the baby without Sayid. She runs up to Sayid and throws her arms around his neck. She knows that he is a very brave man.

✈

As night arrived at sea, Sawyer turned on the radar. Michael told him it was too soon – they needed to save the battery. 'Sayid said we had to turn it on every hour,' Sawyer replied.

Michael changed the subject. He couldn't understand why Sawyer jumped into the water to get the rudder. He could have died. 'You're either very brave or you want to die,' he said.

Their conversation stopped when they heard a noise and saw a small circle of light on the radar's screen. It could only mean one thing. They had found a ship!

They only had one rocket, but Michael thought they should use it. It might be their only chance. He pointed the gun in the air and fired. The rocket lit up the sky.

At first, they thought the ship hadn't seen them. But then they heard the sound of a motor coming towards them. They all stood up and waved. 'Hey, over here!' Michael shouted.

As the motor got closer, a very bright light suddenly shone into their faces. Beyond the light, they saw a group of men. They looked very rough. Michael told them about the plane crash and asked for help.

'Sure, we'll help you,' they shouted. 'But first, give us the boy!'

Michael didn't understand what was happening. Sawyer did. He pulled out his gun, but someone from the other boat fired first. They hit Sawyer in the shoulder and he fell into the sea. Jin jumped in to rescue him.

The rough men jumped onto Michael's boat. They knocked Michael into the water. Then they took Walt and threw some explosives onto Michael's boat. Seconds later, his boat exploded. 'Dad, Dad!' Walt screamed.

In the water, Michael could do nothing. He watched, feeling angry and useless. His boat was sinking as his son disappeared into the night.

✈

At last, Jack's group have arrived at the hatch. Jack and Locke are placing the explosives. Suddenly, Hurley sees a line of numbers on the hatch. They are the numbers that he used to win his money. This can't be good. 'You have to stop!' he shouts. But Locke isn't interested. A few seconds later, there is a huge explosion.

They go back to the hatch. This time it is open. They move the hatch door to one side and look down. Below them lies the beginning of a deep, dark mystery.

THE MAKING OF *LOST*

***Lost* is a hugely successful show. The actors, writers, directors and producers all play a big part in its success. But what about the location and the people who work behind the scenes?**

THE LOCATION

Most of *Lost* was filmed in Hawaii on the island of Oahu, in the Pacific Ocean. Oahu had almost everything the programme needed: forests, beautiful beaches, fish, fruit trees and wild animals. But there were some problems, too:

- The place where the plane crashes is a popular beach called Mokuleia. It has a narrow road going through it. The film company had to cover the road with sand and stop any traffic while they were filming.
- A group of people also lived on the beach. It was difficult moving them and some of them stayed in the film company's camp.
- Sudden rainstorms also made filming difficult.

But Mokuleia is a beautiful place. One of the producers, Sarah Calpan, said, 'We had three weeks of filming at the beach and it was fantastic.'

Mokuleia beach

Filming on the beach

Working in the rain

THE CREW

The crew are the people who work for the directors and the producers behind the scenes. They include the people who work the sound, lighting and cameras and the make-up artists.

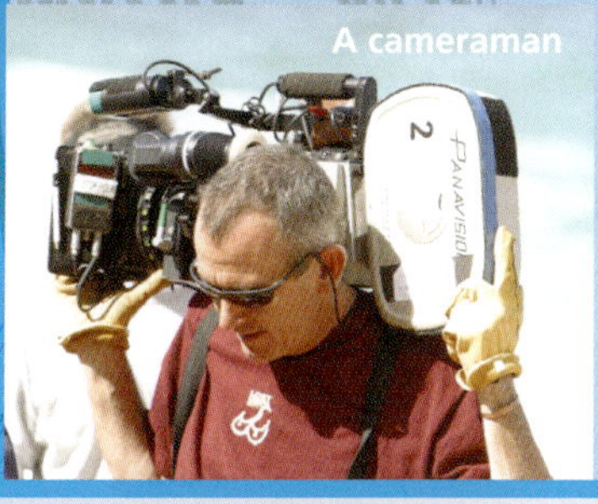

A cameraman

A make-up artist at work

The crew worked really hard to make everything in the show look good and seem real. For example, the make-up artists make the actors look beautiful or handsome – or like they have bad injuries!

THE SPECIAL EFFECTS

A team of special effects people also worked hard to make scenes of mystery and danger even more real. They used computers to add digital images after filming. For example, many of the explosions were added by special effects artists. And green screens are often used in scenes that are too dangerous to film for real.

These pictures show Hurley crossing the rope bridge with the green screen background, and then with the digital image background.

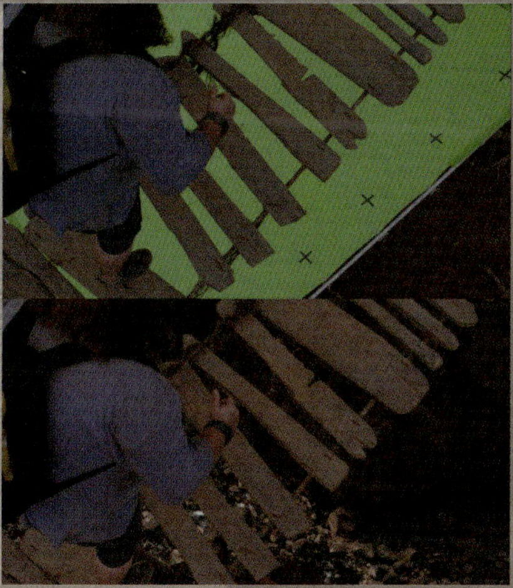

What do these words mean?
You can use a dictionary.
location scene crew
special effects digital image

Would you like to work in TV or films? Which film or TV show would you like to work on? What job would you like to do behind the scenes?

THE CREATORS OF *LOST*

J.J. Abrams and Damon Lindelof, the creators of *Lost*, talked to us about the show.

Lost is a success because you both work well together. Is this true?

Lindelof: It's true for many reasons. The first time I met J.J. he saw me as someone who was working with him and not for him. Also we liked the same movies, the same books and the same magazines.

Abrams: Almost immediately, I saw Damon as a friend. Since that time, working together has been easy. For me, finding someone like Damon was a real gift.

Lost gave you some difficult problems. How did you manage them?

Lindelof: Our main problem was how to make a show about people stuck on an island interesting. So we decided to make it not just about the people. It would be people against nature, people against people and people against the unknown. This meant introducing science-fiction. Also the people would have interesting past lives.

Abrams: So we used the idea of flashbacks. They begin right from the first show when Jack looks back at the moments before the plane crashes.

Lindelof: In this way, the viewers discover who the people are very slowly. Their secrets are as much a mystery as the island.

Lindelof and Abrams

Why did you decide to kill Boone?

Abrams: If we wanted people to believe the series, someone had to die. We decided on Boone because he is often in danger through being with Locke. If they both survived, viewers might feel tricked.

Lindelof: Also, we had used so many false deaths that we had to have at least one real one. For example, Shannon had died but it wasn't real. Then Charlie was hung and Jack and Kate saved him. But Boone might still come back in flashbacks.

Finally, can you say what will happen with *Lost* in the future?

Abrams: The story is driven by viewers' questions. For example, why can Locke walk? Who or what is the huge thing in the forest? Some of these questions will be answered sooner rather than later. But we're not going to give the answers here. The viewers will have to watch the show!

Working with the creators

"I'm from the southern US but when I auditioned for the part of Sawyer, I tried to speak like a New Yorker. I forgot my words, shouted something rude, and kicked a chair across the room. That's when J.J. said, 'That's great. Be yourself. Be southern.' So I got the job."

Josh Holloway (Sawyer)

"Damon likes to say that Jack and Sawyer could have been brothers. The only difference is their family lives. Jack's family was rich and successful. Sawyer's was poor and difficult. But they are similar, under the skin. Maybe that's why they disagree so much."

Matthew Fox (Jack)

"In the scene where I see the huge thing, I asked Damon's advice. 'OK,' I said. 'There's this huge thing coming towards me. I look up, but what do I see?' And Damon answered, 'How about the most beautiful thing you've ever seen in your life?'"

Terry O'Quinn (Locke)

What do these words mean? You can use a dictionary.
creator science-fiction flashback auditioned scene

What do you think is going to happen in *Lost* in the future?

Real-life mysteries ... fact or fiction?

Lost **isn't a true story, but it draws upon some real-life mysteries. We look at two popular mysteries. How can strange things like these happen in the real world?**

'THE MARY CELESTE'

The ship, 'The Mary Celeste', left New York for Italy on 7 November 1872. The captain was a man called Benjamin Briggs. With him were his wife, his young daughter and a crew of seven men. None of them was ever seen again.

Less than a month later, another ship called 'Dei Gratia' found 'The Mary Celeste' on the sea near Portugal. When sailors from 'Dei Gratia' went onto 'The Mary Celeste', they found that breakfast was ready on the table. But there were no people. Everything else was fine. There was money in a wooden box and the ship was carrying a lot of alcohol. There was no sign of an attack and nothing was taken.

Breakfast was ready but there were no people

Had everyone fallen into the sea during an unusual storm? Did a huge sea creature attack them? Did someone kill everyone and then disappear? No answer to this mystery has ever been found.

THE BERMUDA TRIANGLE

The Bermuda Triangle is an area of the Atlantic north of the Caribbean. Many planes and ships have disappeared within this area and have never been seen again.

The famous explorer, Christopher Columbus, first wrote about the area after his journey to the New World. He wrote of seeing 'strange dancing lights on the sea.' In 1838, a ship called 'The Rosalie' was found on the sea without any people on it near the Bahamas. In 1918, the US ship 'Cyclops' disappeared with 309 men. There was no storm and the ship's loss is known as the 'US's greatest mystery at sea.'

In more modern times, planes have also disappeared. The first recorded mystery happened on 5 December 1945. Five US warplanes left from Fort Lauderdale on a training flight. They never returned.

This plane disappeared in December 1945

There are many ideas about the Bermuda Triangle. Some people say that it's a place visited by extra-terrestrials. Others say it's a place where sudden strange weather makes things disappear. Dr Richard McIver has an interesting idea. He explains that there are large areas of gas under the floor of the sea. Sometimes these can rise up through the sea and into the air. As the gas goes down, it can pull things down with it. What do you think?

What do these words mean? You can use a dictionary.
fiction captain crew alcohol loss extra-terrestrial

Can you explain any of these mysteries? Do you know of any other similar mysteries?

PROLOGUE – CHAPTER 4

Before you read

You can use your dictionary.

1 Match these words with their definitions.

hunt trap hatch cave boar camp polar bear

a) A heavy door, usually on a plane or ship.
b) A large hole in a hill or in the ground.
c) To kill or catch animals.
d) A place, usually with tents, where people stay.
e) A large, white animal that lives in the Arctic.
f) A kind of wild pig.

2 Complete the sentences with these words.

drug creature rope unconscious

a) It sounded like a large, dangerous ... coming through the forest.
b) He can't hear or see us. He's not sleeping. He's … .
c) She needs to take a special … for her illness.
d) They used a long … to tie their prisoner to a tree.

After you read

3 Complete the sentences with the correct names.

Michael Sun Ethan Boone

a) ... cut Shannon free.
b) … didn't want Jin to know she spoke English.
c) … spent nine years away from his son.
d) … killed a man called Scott Jackson.

4 What do you think?

a) Is Kate starting to like Sawyer?
b) Is Michael a good father to Walt?
c) Is Michael's boat-building a good idea?
d) Should Locke and Boone tell the others about the hatch?

CHAPTERS 5–8

Before you read

You can use a dictionary.

5 Look at these words.

psychiatric radar breathe explosion battery kidney

Which one …

a) is part of the body?
b) is impossible to do in water?
c) is a type of hospital?
d) finds things you can't see?
e) is loud and dangerous?
f) helps machines to work?

6 Guess the answers to these questions.

a) Chapter 5 is called *Fire on the beach*. What will catch fire?
b) In Chapter 6, Hurley is worried when he sees numbers 4 8 15 16 23 42. Why?
c) Someone will die in Chapters 5–8. Who will it be?
d) Jack wants to find someone at the end of Chapter 8. Who?

Now read Chapters 5–8. Were you right?

After you read

7 Who says these things?

a) 'Why did you burn the boat?'
b) 'I like it here.'
c) 'I just saved your life.'
d) 'I think that the plane crash was my fault.'
e) 'I've done everything you asked.'
f) 'Locke told me not to tell anyone.'
g) 'Just let me go.'
h) 'He was murdered.'

8 Put these parts of the story in the right order.
a) Claire has her baby.
b) Jin burns his arms.
c) Boone dies.
d) A light shines through the hatch.
e) Danielle's camp is destroyed.
f) Sun screams in English.

CHAPTERS 9–12

Before you read

9 What do you think? True or false?
a) Sayid thinks Boone was a brave man.
b) Jack kills Locke.
c) Michael's boat finds a ship to rescue them.
d) Jack and the others find 'The Black Rock'
e) Kate makes Michael ill.
Now read Chapters 9–12. Were you right?

After you read

10 Answer these questions.
a) Why does Sun not want Jin to go on the boat?
b) Who always comes at night?
c) What do they want to get from 'The Black Rock'?
d) What kind of ship was 'The Black Rock'?
e) What does Danielle take from Claire?

11 What do you think?
a) Kate took Joanna's passport. Did she do the right thing?
b) Is Sawyer mainly good or bad?
c) Who are the people on the other boat?
d) Why does Hurley shout, 'You have to stop.'
e) What will happen to Walt? Will Michael be able to rescue him?